D1325375

A PARRAGON BOOK

Published by Parragon Book Service Ltd,
Units 13-17, Avonbridge Trading Estate, Atlantic Road,
Avonmouth, Bristol BS11 9QD

Produced by The Templar Company plc,
Pippbrook Mill, London Road, Dorking,
Surrey RH4 1JE

Written by Robert Snedden
Series Editor Robert Snedden
Designed by Mark Summersby
Illustrations by Peter Bull Art Studio

Printed and bound in the UK

ISBN 0 7525 1667 1

·PARRAGON·

CONTENTS

EXPLORING THE UNIVERSE

We are going on a journey that will take us towards the end of space and the beginning of time. We will start with our own planet Earth, extraordinary and unique, as far as we know, and continue on to explore our neighbouring planets in the Solar System. We will cross vast depths of space to the stars and leap across the void to far-off galaxies. On the way we will see some of the marvels of the Universe, including the mysterious high-energy quasars and the awesome black holes.

We will not be the first to take this journey. Astronomy, the study of everything that lies beyond the Earth's atmosphere, is perhaps the most ancient of all the sciences. For thousands of years, ever since the first dawning of intelligence, humans have looked up into the night sky and wondered about what they saw there. Thousands of years ago people found patterns in the stars and named them after their gods and heroes. They saw stories and myths mirrored in the sky above them.

Observers began to watch the Sun, Moon and stars and link their movements to events on the Earth. The rising and setting of the Sun marked the passing of a day; the phases of the Moon from full to new and back to full took a month, and as the year progressed different groups of stars appeared in the sky as the seasons moved on through spring to summer, autumn and winter and back to spring again. Some people even came to believe that the positions of the stars, and especially the wandering stars they called planets, could affect what happened to individuals here on Earth.

Over the centuries many great minds have turned their attentions to the exploration and understanding of the Universe beyond the Earth. The more we have discovered, the further out the boundaries of space have been pushed. From the ancient belief that the Earth was at the centre of the Universe we have come to see ourselves as a tiny speck somewhere in the midst of an expanding cosmos that is vast beyond all comprehension.

Today we have powerful tools at our disposal. We can explore space in ways undreamed of by the people of long ago, or even by astronomers living in the last century. As well as improving the range of our eyes with telescopes, both on Earth and in space, we also use invisible radiation such as radio waves and x-rays to open up the secrets of the Universe. Sometimes, however, we still have to use one of the most powerful tools of all, a tool that the ancients also had. It is called imagination and it can take us anywhere.

THE EARTH

As planets go the Earth is fairly average. Its 12,700 km (8000 miles) diameter is three times that of tiny Pluto but less than a tenth that of the giant planet Jupiter.

The Earth is 150 million km (93,750,000 miles) from the Sun, which, luckily for us, puts it at just the right temperature for there to be liquid water. For all we know there may be unknown forms of life elsewhere in the Universe that can live without water, but there are none on our planet.

A blanket of gases, called the atmosphere, surrounds the Earth and protects its surface. The atmosphere lets sunlight through, but other, more harmful, rays are filtered out. All but the largest meteors are burned up in the atmosphere before they reach the surface. And, of course, without the atmosphere we couldn't breathe!

The first travellers to the Moon could look back and see the Earth shining brightly in space. This beautiful blue-and-white world is unique because it is the only planet we know of that can support life.

THE MOON

The Moon orbits the Earth at a distance of around 384,000 km (240,000 miles). It is 3476 km (2160 miles) in diameter, less than a third as big as our planet.

Although it is by far the brightest object in the night sky the Moon produces no light of its own. We can only see it because it reflects light from the Sun.

The Moon keeps the same side turned towards us as it orbits the Earth. We can only see it when it is lit up by the Sun.

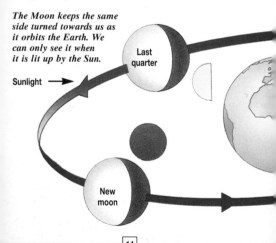

Sunlight ⟶

Last quarter

New moon

A day on the Moon lasts about 27 Earth days. This is also the time it takes for the Moon to travel around the Earth. We always see the same side of the Moon from the Earth. When the night-time side is towards us it is invisible from Earth.

The surface of the Moon is covered by craters, some around 200 km (125 miles) across. These great scars were caused by large meteorites striking the Moon at great speeds. There is no atmosphere to protect it.

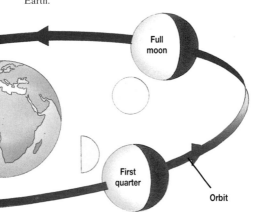

Full moon

First quarter

Orbit

THE SUN

The Sun is like a massive nuclear reactor, pouring out huge quantities of heat and light. For us on Earth, it is the most important object in space, keeping our planet warm enough for life to exist.

Every second, four million tonnes of the Sun's mass are converted into energy. But it won't burn away altogether – the Sun weighs around 2000 million million million tonnes, so it should last a bit longer, probably around five billion years!

The Sun is almost 1,400,000 km (865,000 miles across), 100 times the diameter of the Earth.

The temperature at the surface of the Sun is 5500°C (9900°F), rising to 14 million°C (25 million°F) at the centre.

Dark patches, called sunspots, can sometimes be seen on the surface of the Sun. Measuring tens of thousands of kilometres across, sunspots are a couple of thousand degrees cooler than the surrounding surface.

In the heart of the Sun atomic reactions fuse hydrogen, the lightest element, into heavier elements, releasing energy.

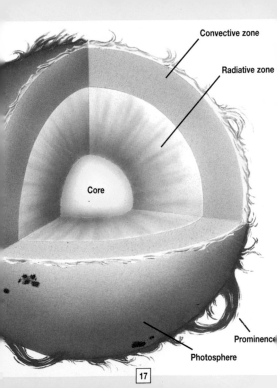

Convective zone

Radiative zone

Core

Prominence

Photosphere

THE SOLAR SYSTEM

The Sun and all the multitude of objects in orbit around it together make up the Solar System. The Sun lies at the heart of a family of nine planets and their moons, plus millions of asteroids, comets and other objects.

Ninety-nine per cent of the mass of the Solar System is contained within the Sun.

Starting with the closest to the Sun, the nine planets are: Mercury, Venus, Earth, Mars, Jupiter, Saturn, Uranus, Neptune and Pluto. Between Mars

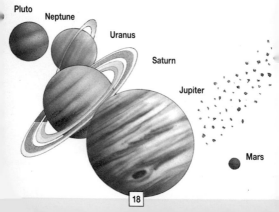

Pluto

Neptune

Uranus

Saturn

Jupiter

Mars

and Jupiter lies the Asteroid Belt, where most of these minor planets are to be found. Beyond Pluto, far out towards the outer reaches of the Solar System, is the Oort Cloud, a vast spherical cloud of comets left over from the formation of the Sun and planets, that surrounds the Solar System. The distance from the Sun to the Oort Cloud may be between 10 and 20 million million km (6 and 12 million million miles)!

In this plan of the Solar System the sizes of the planets are to scale, but not the distances between them.

Mercury

Asteroid Belt

Venus

Earth

MERCURY

The closest planet to the Sun is Mercury, the second smallest planet in the Solar System after Pluto. At an average distance of 58 million km (36 million miles), Mercury takes just 88 Earth days to complete one orbit of the Sun. A 'day' on Mercury lasts 156 Earth days, or almost two Mercury years!

For three months one side of Mercury is turned towards the Sun. Temperatures rise to 420°C (800°F) at midday, hot enough to melt lead and certainly far too hot for there to be any life on Mercury. After the Sun sets and the long Mercurian night begins the temperature falls to -180°C (-300°F), a drop of 600C° (1100F°)!

Mercury has no atmosphere to protect it from these drastic temperature changes, nor from meteorite bombardment. When the space probe Mariner 10 sent back pictures of the planet in 1974 it revealed a surface covered by craters.

Mercury is an inhospitable planet. Three times nearer the Sun than the Earth is, its airless, cratered surface is baked by heat and radiation.

VENUS

Venus is the planet that comes nearest to the Earth. At its closest approach it is around 42 million km (26 million miles) from us.

Venus is also the closest planet to the Earth in terms of size. It is only slightly smaller, at 12,100 km (7500 miles) across. In other respects, however, it is a very different planet.

A dense atmosphere of poisonous gases surrounds Venus, hiding its surface from view. Some of the gases in the atmosphere trap the heat from the Sun, making the surface of Venus a baking hot 480°C (900°F), even hotter than Mercury. Sulphuric acid clouds make Venus even more unpleasant.

Venus is sometimes called the Evening Star because it can be seen shining brightly in the sky just after sunset. Only the Sun and Moon are brighter.

Astronomers have found evidence of volcanic activity on the barren surface of Venus.

MARS

Travelling out into the Solar System beyond the Earth the first planet we come to is Mars. Mars is one of the smaller planets, just 6726 km (4180 miles across), about half the size of the Earth, but it has the biggest volcano in the Solar System, the 26-km (16-mile) high Olympus Mons, three times the height of Mount Everest.

Mars is sometimes called the Red Planet from its appearance in the sky. Only a thin atmosphere protects its surface and the average temperature is a chilly -23°C (-10°F). At one time it was believed that there might be intelligent life on Mars. It is probable that millions of years ago Mars was warmer and there were

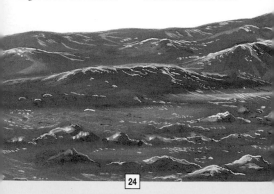

oceans there, and possibly some form of life as well, but we can find no traces of it now.

Mars has two tiny, irregularly-shaped moons, Phobos and Deimos. These are probably asteroids that were captured by the planet.

The Viking space probes, which reached Mars in 1976, split into an orbiter and a lander. The orbiters mapped the surface of Mars and the landers analysed the Martian atmosphere and soil. They also searched for evidence of life, but found none.

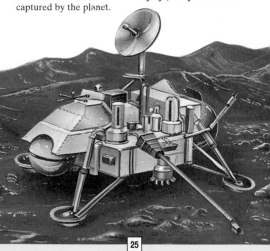

THE ASTEROIDS

In the eighteenth century astronomers felt certain that there should be another planet between Mars and Jupiter and began to search for the missing world.

In 1801 the first asteroid, Ceres, was discovered. A mere 933 km (580 miles) across it was too small to be called a planet. Soon more asteroids were discovered – over 5000 have now been catalogued and there may be millions. Space probes on the way to the outer reaches of the Solar

System have detected many more, some scarcely bigger than sand grains.

Not all of the asteroids orbit between Mars and Jupiter. Some follow long ellipses that take them across the orbit of the Earth and in towards the Sun. Icarus gets closer to the Sun than Mercury, approaching to within 29 million km (18 million miles). The most distant asteroid yet discovered is Chiron, orbiting between Saturn and Uranus.

The asteroids are debris left over from the formation of the Solar System. It is thought that the gravity of massive Jupiter prevented them collecting together to form a planet.

Jupiter, the largest member of the Sun's family, is a gigantic ball of gas and liquid 142,984 km (88,784 miles) in diameter. It is 1500 times larger than the Earth and three times more massive than all the other planets put together. A rocky core is hidden deep beneath Jupiter's surface.

Giant Jupiter is so huge that even its largest moon is bigger than the planet Mercury. Three others are bigger than Pluto!

28

Jupiter spins very fast – a 'day' there lasts just under ten hours. Mighty storms rage in Jupiter's upper atmosphere, powered by the fast rotation of the planet. One storm, the Great Red Spot, is three times the size of the Earth and was first seen over 300 years ago. There are no signs of it dying down!

Sixteen moons and a thin ring of icy particles orbit Jupiter. The four largest moons, Europa, Io, Callisto and Ganymede were first seen by the great Italian astronomer Galileo Galilei in 1610. The Galilean moons, as they are called, are practically worlds in their own right – each one is larger than the planet Pluto. Io is the only place in the Solar System outside the Earth where active volcanoes have been seen.

SATURN

Saturn, another gas giant world, is twice as far from the Sun as Jupiter. It is 100 times more massive than the Earth but if you could drop Saturn in an immense pond it would float!

Saturn's magnificent ring system makes it one of the most spectacular objects in space. It also has more moons than any other planet.

Seen through a telescope Saturn's rings make it one of the most beautiful objects in the night sky. As the space probe

Voyager 2 neared Saturn in 1980, it showed that the rings were divided into smaller ringlets, and those into yet more ringlets. The ringlets are made up mainly of chunks of ice. The total mass of the rings is about equal to that of a medium-sized moon and one theory is that the rings were formed when one of Saturn's moons was torn apart.

Uranus is twice as far from the Sun as Saturn. It is so far from the Earth that it cannot be seen with the naked eye. It was discovered in 1781 by William Herschel. Uranus is odd in that it spins on its side in relation to its path around the Sun.

Astronomers knew little about Uranus until 1986 when Voyager 2 approached the planet. The probe's cameras sent back images of clouds and the scientists were able to time the winds at the top of Uranus's atmosphere at 700 km/h (440 mph). Ten small, previously unknown, moons were also discovered, bringing Uranus's total to 15.

The moon Miranda is one of the most fascinating sights in the Solar System. Its surface is a massive jumble of huge cliffs and ridges. Some astronomers think that an enormous meteorite may have smashed into Miranda, breaking it up into pieces that continued to orbit Uranus. Gravity then gradually pulled the bits back together again, but out of order!

Uranus and its thin ring system as seen from a point in space near its moon Miranda. The planet is tilted on its side in relation to its path around the Sun.

NEPTUNE

Since its discovery in 1846, Neptune had appeared as just a faint blue disc in even the most powerful telescopes. Then, in 1989, after 12 years of travelling through space, Voyager 2 at last reached the planet, 4.5 billion km (2.8 billion miles) out from the Sun. Neptune was revealed as a giant blue planet with the fastest winds in the Solar System. They rip through Neptune's atmosphere at up to 2000 km/h (1250 mph) and blow up huge storms. One such storm, the Great Dark Spot, is as big as the Earth itself. Below the storm astronomers saw a smaller white cloud being blown around Neptune. They called it 'Scooter'.

Neptune has eight moons, only two of which had been seen prior to Voyager 2's visit. Triton, the largest of Neptune's moons, may be the coldest place in the Solar System. Its surface temperature is about -235°C (-455°F).

The Voyager 2 space probe approaching Neptune. The Voyagers sent back a wealth of information on the Solar System's outer planets.

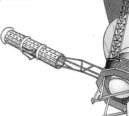

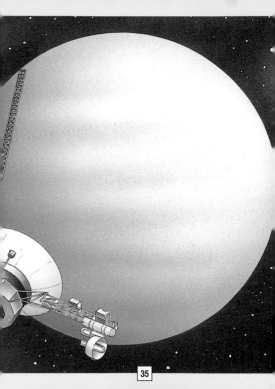

PLUTO

Pluto is the smallest planet in the Solar System and the one that travels furthest from the Sun. It takes 249 years to complete one orbit and at its greatest distance it is over 7 billion km (4 billion miles) out. Its orbit is so eccentric that sometimes it passes inside the orbit of Neptune. In fact, until 1999, Neptune is the furthest planet from the Sun. No space probe has yet visited Pluto and very little is known about what its surface may look like.

Pluto was first found in 1930 and in 1978 astronomers discovered that it has a moon, named Charon, which is nearly half Pluto's size. Astronomers often call the Pluto-Charon pair a 'double planet'.

It took the Hubble space telescope, orbiting above Earth's atmosphere, to show Pluto and Charon as two separate bodies. They are so small and so far away that Earth-based telescopes show them as a single fuzzy ball.

Pluto and its moon, Charon, are more like a double planet. Very little indeed is known about them as no space probe has yet gone there.

COMETS

Out beyond the orbit of Pluto lies the Oort Cloud, a vast cloud of material left over from the formation of the Sun and planets. Occasionally a passing star disturbs part of the cloud and icy objects several kilometres across come spiralling inwards towards the distant Sun.

In the warmer central Solar System radiation from the Sun causes the icy outer layers of the object to boil off into space. They form an immense tail of gas and dust, perhaps 100 million km (60 million miles) long, stretching out from the central body to provide a spectacular night-time display if the object is well-placed for observation from Earth.

This visitor from the outer reaches of the Solar System is a comet. Comets may only be seen once before returning to the Oort Cloud, but from time to time they are captured by the gravity of the planets and take up new orbits in the inner Solar System.

Nucleus

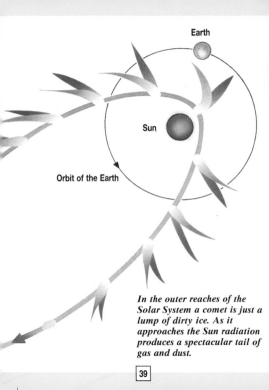

Earth

Sun

Orbit of the Earth

In the outer reaches of the Solar System a comet is just a lump of dirty ice. As it approaches the Sun radiation produces a spectacular tail of gas and dust.

Sometimes, as you look up into the night sky, you may see a streak of light shoot across against the starry background. This 'shooting star' is actually a meteor, a piece of rocky material burning up as it collides with the Earth's atmosphere.

You are more likely to see meteors at certain times of the year than at others. There are huge numbers of particles, called meteoroids, ranging in size from specks of dust to small rocks, orbiting the Sun. The greatest concentrations of particles are found in the tails of comets and it is when the Earth passes through a comet's tail that the most spectacular displays occur.

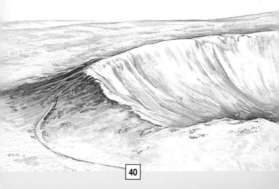

Occasionally a meteoroid that is large enough to survive its fiery passage through the air strikes the atmosphere. A meteoroid that reaches the ground is called a meteorite. One of the largest meteorite craters visible on Earth is Meteor Crater in Arizona, USA. It is 175 metres (575 feet) deep

Meteor Crater in Arizona was formed about 40,000 years ago when a 65-tonne meteorite struck. Some scientists have speculated that a giant meteorite striking the Earth 65 million years ago may have been partly responsible for the extinction of the dinosaurs.

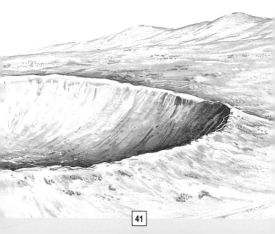

STAR BIRTH

Like all other stars, the Sun began its life in a huge spinning cloud of gas and dust. There are many such dark clouds, called nebulae, scattered through space.

The matter in the nebulae is more or less evenly distributed but sometimes denser patches may form. A nearby supernova explosion or the radiation from young, hot stars close by might push some of the gas and dust together. Gravity causes the growing clump of matter to collapse further, drawing in more material from the cloud.

As the matter in the cloud becomes more and more concentrated the temperature begins to rise. If it reaches around 10 million°C (18 million°F) nuclear reactions begin within the core of the new star. These reactions convert hydrogen, the lightest, and most common, of all elements in the Universe, into other, heavier, elements. The energy produced by these reactions makes the star shine and also stops it from collapsing further.

Star nurseries are vast swirling clouds of gas and dust in space. Sometimes the dust may contain material from older stars that have come to the end of their lives. Planets may also form around the new stars from the same reservoir of matter.

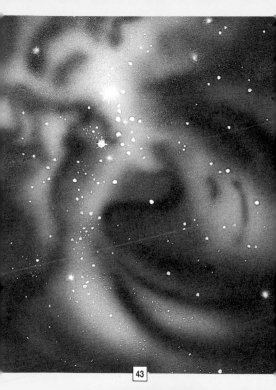

MAIN SEQUENCE

The Hertzsprung-Russell diagram, named after the two astronomers who devised it, classifies stars according to their temperature and brightness. Blue stars, classed as O-types, are the brightest and hottest whereas M-types are cooler and red.

Most stars lie within a narrow band on the diagram that is known as the Main Sequence. The Sun is a typical Main Sequence star. These stars are currently in the hydrogen-burning stage of their lives.

Stars like the Sun will spend about ten billion years on the Main Sequence. Large stars burn faster whereas small stars take longer to use up

their hydrogen. When a star's hydrogen is used up it leaves the Main

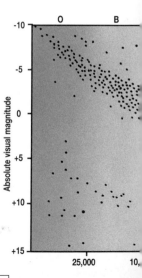

Sequence. What happens to it next depends on how massive it is. The Sun, for example, will first become a red giant before ending its life as a white dwarf.

The Hertzsprung-Russell diagram charts star types according to surface temperature and magnitude, or brightness. The Sun is a G-class star.

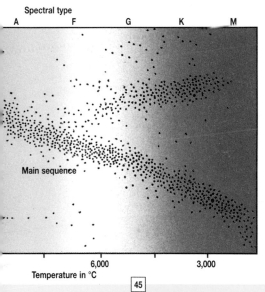

Spectral type

A   F   G   K   M

Main sequence

6,000   3,000

Temperature in °C

RED GIANTS

When a star's hydrogen fuel begins to run out there is no longer sufficient energy to resist gravity and the star contracts. Its core becomes more and more compressed and this causes the temperature of the core to increase. The sudden surge of energy forces the star's outer layers to expand, perhaps to 100 times their original diameter.

The outer layers cool as they expand, dropping to temperatures of around 3,500°C (6,300°F) and the star becomes a red giant. This is what will happen to the Sun in around 5000 million years from now. The expanding outer layers may come out far enough swallow up the Earth itself.

The temperature in the core of a giant star can reach 100 million°C (180 million°F). This is high enough for other, heavier elements to be used as atomic fuel. Eventually, however, the star will run out of usable fuel and the nuclear reactions will cease. Now there is nothing to stop it shrinking and the star collapses and cools.

One of the largest red giant stars in the sky is Betelguese in the constellation of Orion. This supergiant is between 400 and 600 times bigger than the Sun. If Betelguese were in the centre of the Solar System instead of the Sun it would swallow up all the planets out to Mars!

46

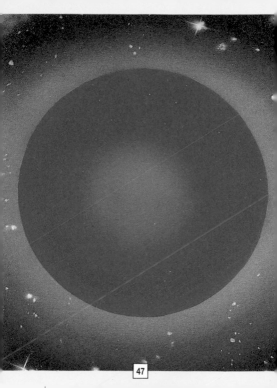

PLANETARY NEBULAE

Red giant stars may throw off their outer layers altogether. These escape into space to form an expanding shell of gas around the star. This is called a planetary nebula, because many give the appearance of discs when seen through a telescope.

When the star loses its outer layers the hot inner regions are exposed. Huge amounts of high-energy ultraviolet radiation pour out from the newly revealed surface, which may be at a temperature of 100,000°C (180,000°F) or more. This radiation is absorbed by the gas in the surrounding planetary nebula and some of it is re-emitted as light, making the nebula visible from Earth.

Planetary nebulae have a short lifetime in astronomical terms. They last only a few tens of thousands of years before the material drifts off into interstellar space and becomes too rarified to be seen.

Millions of years after it has dispersed, the remains of a planetary nebula may form part of interstellar gas clouds that will form new stars.

A planetary nebula is an expanding envelope of gas and dust surrounding a hot central star. Radiation from the star makes the dust glow. The cloud expands at a few tens of metres per second and will be dispersed into interstellar space within 100,000 years.

WHITE DWARVES

The central part of a star left behind when a planetary nebula drifts off into space cools and contracts until it is about the size of the Earth. A star that was less than 1.4 times more massive than the Sun then settles down into a long existence at the end of its stellar life as a white dwarf.

White dwarfs are faint and difficult to detect. Often, however, one will form part of a binary system. The powerful gravity of the white dwarf pulls in material from its companion star and when this strikes the surface of the dwarf star nuclear reactions may start up again, causing the dwarf star to shine brightly for a time. We then see it as a nova.

A white dwarf continues to shine as gravitational energy, released as it collapes, is turned into heat and light. Eventually, however, this

source of energy runs out
and the star becomes a
dark black dwarf.

**Material is pulled from the companion
star by the white dwarf.**

**Material striking
the surface of the
dwarf star causes
it to flare up.**

*Sometimes a white dwarf
star will be revealed to
astronomers by the effect
it has on a nearby
companion star. Material
sucked in from the
companion makes the
dwarf flare up brightly.*

SUPERNOVAS

When a giant star that is several times more massive than the Sun runs out of nuclear fuel its core contracts and becomes unimaginably hot. The outer layers implode violently as the star's powerful gravity pulls them inwards. The enormous temperatures and pressures this produces cause the outer layers to ricochet back from the dense core, blowing them right off into space.

For a short time the exploding star, or supernova, as it is called, can outshine all the other stars in its galaxy. In just a few moments a supernova can produce as much energy as the Sun will in its entire life! Astronomers believe that a supernova occurs somewhere in our galaxy about once every thirty years or so.

What eventually happens to the super-dense collapsed core that remains after the explosion will depend on how massive the star was to begin with.

A supernova is a catastrophic stellar explosion that sends colossal amounts of matter and energy streaming into space. We can see the remains of a supernova as a bright expanding nebula that emits radiation in many different forms including radio waves, light and x-rays. Supernovae enrich space with heavier elements, including some necessary for life.

NEUTRON STARS

After the supernova explosion of a star around three times more massive than the Sun all that is left is a tiny collapsed core about 25km (15 miles) across. This is a neutron star. In its unbelievably compacted interior the very atoms are crushed together. Just a spoonful of material from a neutron star would weigh more than a billion tonnes on Earth.

As the star collapses in on itself it spins faster and faster and the magnetic field that surrounds it becomes more concentrated and powerful. Particles within the magnetic field are accelerated to nearly the speed of light and streams of radiation shoot out from the star's north and south poles. Because it no longer gives off light, we can only detect the star when one of these streams points towards the Earth. The star appears to pulse rapidly as the beams sweep by like the beams from a lighthouse. Such stars are called pulsars.

Direction of rotation of neutron star

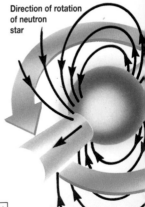

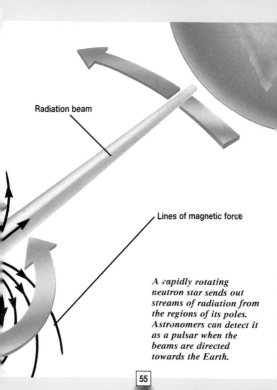

Radiation beam

Lines of magnetic force

A rapidly rotating neutron star sends out streams of radiation from the regions of its poles. Astronomers can detect it as a pulsar when the beams are directed towards the Earth.

BLACK HOLES

What happens to a star that is very much more massive than the Sun? The gravity of a star of over eight times the mass of the Sun would be more powerful than the particles within it could resist once all the nuclear reactions had ceased. The star would keep on collapsing past the neutron star stage until it appeared to vanish altogether! Its gravity would become so power-fully concentrated that not even light could escape from it. There would be only a black hole in space.

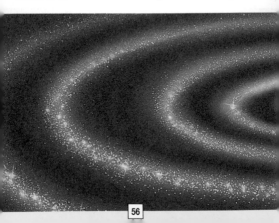

It is impossible, of course, to see a black hole. However, astronomers believe that one member of the binary star Cygnus X-1 is a black hole and the Hubble Space Telescope may have detected evidence of a colossal black hole three trillion times more massive than the Sun at the centre of a distant galaxy.

Nothing, not even light, can escape a black hole. The only way to detect one is by its effects on other objects in space. Radiation may be produced near the hole as particles are ripped apart by its gravity or we may see deviations in the movements of stars as their paths take them close to a black hole

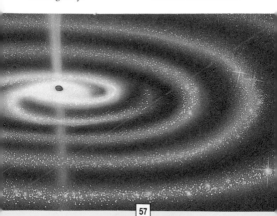

MULTIPLE STARS

Often two stars appear very close together in the night sky. These pairs of stars are called binaries. Sometimes the stars only seem to be close together because they lie in the same direction. and in fact, they are far apart. These stars are called optical binaries.

However, many stars do form small groups of two or more, in orbit around each other like the planets orbit the Sun. Around half the stars in the Universe are members of multiples such as this.

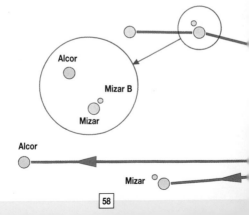

Alcor

Mizar B

Mizar

Alcor

Mizar

The closest star to Earth, Proxima Centauri, is one member of a triple-star system. Some multiple systems can be quite complex, with several binary stars in orbit around each other.

Some binaries are so close to each other that material streams from one star to another. One pair is known where the stars are so close together that they hurtle around each other in just over 11 minutes!

The stars Mizar and Alcor in the constellation of Ursa Major form an optical binary because they appear close together in the sky when seen from the Earth. Mizar itself is actually a double system and Mizar B may even be a triple star system!

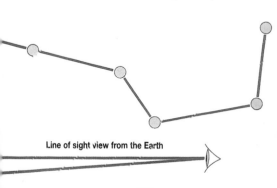

Line of sight view from the Earth

STAR CLUSTERS

It is not uncommon to find stars gathered together in compact groups called clusters. There are two types of cluster. Open clusters are irregular in shape and may contain anything from a dozen to a few hundred stars. All of the stars in the cluster will have formed at around the same time from the same cloud of gas and dust.

Globular clusters may have a hundred thousand or more individual stars. Gravitational attractions between the stars keep the cluster tightly packed, with stars as little as half a light-year apart at the centre.

Globular clusters are most often found around the outside of even larger concentrations of stars – the galaxies. The clusters form a sphere or halo around the main body of the galaxy.

The stars in globular clusters are among the oldest known and are thought to have formed at the same time as the galaxies they are part of.

Globular star clusters of more than a hundred thousand tightly packed stars may be found in haloes around galaxies. Imagine what the night sky would look like from the centre of such a cluster! Possibly they formed from material left over from the formation of the galaxies they surround just as planets may form from the remnants of star formation.

THE MILKY WAY

On a clear night, where there are no streetlights to interfere with the view, a faint band of light is visible stretching across the night sky. This is the Milky Way. If you have the chance to look at the Milky Way through binoculars you will discover that it is made up of a vast number of stars.

The Sun is just one of around 200 billion stars that together make up a great star system called the Galaxy. The Milky Way is what we see when we look towards the main

concentration of stars in the Galaxy. The Galaxy is almost 100,000 light-years across and just over 3000 light-years thick in the centre. A spherical cloud of stars, some 100,000 light-years across, surrounds the Galaxy. Within this cloud can be found globular clusters and some of the oldest stars in the Galaxy.

The Milky Way Galaxy is like a huge city of stars. It is shaped like a thin disc with arms of stars spiralling out from a central bulging nucleus, where most of the stars in the Galaxy are found. The Sun is located in one of the arms in the outer part of the Milky Way, some way out in the galactic suburbs!

GALAXIES

The Milky Way is just one of perhaps more than 100 billion galaxies in the known Universe, each of them containing 100 billion stars or more. That makes over 10,000 billion billion stars in the Universe!

All galaxies rotate, with each star in orbit around the centre. The Sun takes 220 million years to go once around the Galaxy.

The distances between galaxies are mind-boggling. The nearest large galaxy to the Milky Way is the Andromeda Galaxy and yet even this is so distant that light from it takes over two million years to reach us. The light from the furthest galaxies set out on its journey across the Universe billions of years before the Earth was formed!

There are several types of galaxy. Some are spirals, like the Milky Way and the Andromeda Galaxy. Some spirals appear to start at the end of bars of stars that protrude from the central galactic hub. These are called barred spirals. Other galaxies are irregular in shape. The most common are the elliptical galaxies, which have a uniform shape with no spiral arms. Ellipticals are made up almost entirely of old red stars.

Over 100 billion galaxies scattered through the Universe. The Andromeda Galaxy, one of our nearest neighbours, is a spiral galaxy like our own.

GALACTIC CLUSTERS

Like stars, galaxies are not usually found alone in space but tend to be members of groups. Our Milky Way Galaxy and the Andromeda Galaxy are both members of the Local Group of about two dozen galaxies. Andromeda is twice as big as the Milky Way and the largest member of the Local Group.

The Local Group, in turn, lies on the edge of a vast system called the Local Supercluster, which is made up of some dozens of groups of galaxies. The Virgo Cluster, the main component of the Local Supercluster, contains thousands of galaxies.

Other superclusters have also been charted. Recently astronomers discovered a vast chain of galaxies stretching across 500 million light-years of space. This colossal cosmic structure has been called the Great Wall.

Between the superclusters there are great gulfs of nearly empty space which have been called the voids. The structure of the Universe may be something like a froth of bubbles with the super-clusters on the surface and the empty voids in the middle.

Galaxies appear to exist together in great clusters stretching across the Universe. Astronomers are still trying to come to an understanding of how these unimaginably vast structures could have come into being.

QUASARS

Quasars are extraordinary high-energy objects. Many are located in the farthest known reaches of the Universe and are among the remotest objects yet detected. The most distant quasar is around 13,000 million light-years away!

A quasar emits enormous amounts of energy, perhaps as much as a hundred times that of a galaxy! Yet all this power seems to emanate from a region of space not much bigger than the Solar System.

What could be providing all this power? Astronomers believe that giant black holes, millions of times more massive than the Sun, may lurk at the heart of quasars. The black hole sucks in material which heats up and gives off a prodigious amount of energy as the black hole rips its constituent atoms apart.

When we look at quasars we must remember that, because their light takes so long to reach us, we are looking into the distant past. It is possible that quasars may represent some early stage in the evolution of galaxies and were common features of the early Universe.

Quasars are among the most distant and the most highly energetic of all objects in the Universe. They may be powered by supermassive black holes at the cores of very young galaxies in the process of formation.

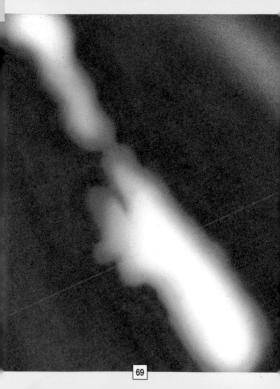

THE BIG BANG

One of the greatest of astronomical discoveries was that the Universe is expanding. Wherever we look in space we see that the galaxies are rushing apart. The most distant quasars appear to be receding from us at around 90 per cent of the speed of light! Why should this be so?

If, in our imaginations, we reverse this process we must conclude that at one time in the distant past all of the material in

the Universe was concentrated in a single point. Most astronomers now believe that there was a 'big bang' that caused the Universe to fly apart. In the first fraction of a second of its existence the Universe must have been pure energy as temperatures would have been far too high for matter to exist. As it cooled, the first particles formed. Over time these would gather together, forming the superclusters, galaxies, stars, planets – and us.

What happened before the Big Bang is an impossble question – as time and space did not exist there was no before!

CONSTELLATIONS

Almost since people first began to observe the stars they have divided them up into groups. These constellations were often given the names of mythical beings and heroes, such as Orion the Hunter and Pegasus the Winged Horse.

We now know that the stars in a constellation have no real relationship with each other. They simply happen to lie in the same line-of-sight direction when observed from the Earth and the individual stars in a constellation may actually be hundreds of light-years apart.

However, present-day astronomers still use constellations as a convenient way of dividing up the sky and locating objects. There are 88 recognised constellations and every astronomical object outside the Solar System can be assigned to one of these regions. For example the Andromeda Galaxy lies within the constellation of Andromeda, although it is, of course, at a very much greater distance than any of the stars that make up that grouping.

Modern day astronomers, following an ancient tradition, divide the night sky into different regions called constellations. This is the constellation of Orion the Hunter. It is one of the most clearly visible constellations in the winter sky above the Northern Hemisphere.

TELESCOPES

Telescopes are the tools of the astronomer's trade. They allow us to see further out into space than we could possibly do otherwise. There are two main types of optical telescope – the refracting telescope and the reflecting telescope. The refracting telescope, which was the first to be invented, uses a lens to gather and focus light to produce an image of a distant object. The reflecting telescope uses a large mirror to collect the light, rather than a lens. A smaller mirror then reflects the light to an eyepiece where the image can be seen. Reflecting telescopes can be made much bigger, and therefore more powerful, than refracting telescopes. Catadioptric telescopes use a combination of mirrors and lenses. They are lightweight and portable, making them a

REFRACTOR

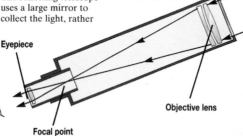

Eyepiece

Objective lens

Focal point

popular choice for amateur astronomers.

Radio telescopes do not use light at all. They detect the radio waves that are given out by many objects in space.

They allow astronomers to examine objects that would otherwise be hidden.

These diagrams show the three types of optical telescope.

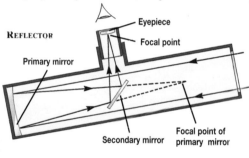

REFLECTOR

Eyepiece

Focal point

Primary mirror

Secondary mirror

Focal point of primary mirror

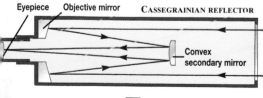

Eyepiece

Objective mirror

CASSEGRAINIAN REFLECTOR

Convex secondary mirror

OBSERVATORIES

Large telescopes are housed in specially constructed buildings called observatories. Because the sky is not totally dark, even at night, the siting of a large telescope is more important than its size. Observatories are usually built high up on mountains, away from pollution and city lights that would make observations more difficult.

The production of mirrors and lenses for very large telescopes is a costly and time-consuming business and it may be shared by several countries, which will then use the facilities. The largest telescope in use at present is a six-metre (236-inch) reflector in the Caucasus Mountains, Russia.

Radio telescope observatories can be spread over large areas. There may be several radio dishes linked together working in unison to provide a single radio 'picture'. The Very Large Array in New Mexico, USA, has a series of 27 individually movable radio telescopes spread out along railway tracks in a Y-shape. Each arm of the Y is 21km (13 miles) long.

The Very Large Array in New Mexico is a series of linked mobile radio telescopes.

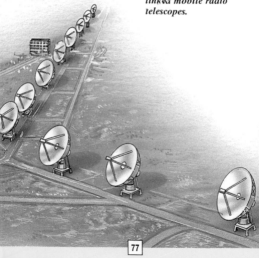

The only way to carry out astronomical observations away from the distorting effects of the Earth's atmosphere is to send telescopes into space. Over the past few decades telescopes and other instruments capable of examining the Universe using infra-red, ultra-violet, x-rays and visible light have been launched into orbit around the Earth.

The Infrared Astronomical Satellite (IRAS), launched in 1983, made some surprising discoveries. Among the things it detected were clouds of debris around some stars, suggesting that planetary systems, similar to the Solar System, have formed elsewhere in space.

The Hubble Space Telescope was launched in 1990. After some initial difficulties involving a faulty mirror, since repaired by astronauts from the space shuttle, Hubble has been producing some of the most spectacular and revealing pictures of deep space yet seen, including star nurseries. It should eventually be able to show us objects more than 60 million times fainter than any that can be seen from Earth with the naked eye!

The Hubble Space Telescope, named after the American astronomer Edwin Hubble, who first showed that the Universe is expanding, has produced some of the most extra-ordinary images of objects in space ever seen.

SPACE PROBES

Whereas satellites stay in orbit around the Earth, space probes are like artificial explorers sent out to investigate other parts of the Solar System. They can get to places that would be too difficult or costly for a human team to reach.

Probes have been sent into orbit around Mercury, Venus and Mars and to intercept comets. They have plunged into the atmosphere of Jupiter and landed on the surfaces of Venus and Mars. They have all returned valuable information about conditions on these planets that we could not have obtained otherwise. The only planet not yet visited by a probe from Earth is Pluto, but a mission is being planned.

Of all the probes that have been dispatched so far, Voyagers 1 and 2, both launched in 1977, have provided the most exciting results. Both craft flew by

Jupiter in 1979 and Saturn in 1980 and 1981. Voyager 2 continued on to Uranus in 1986 and Neptune in 1989. Wonderful pictures, revealing never before seen details of these planets and their moons were sent back to Earth.

The Giotto probe flew past Halley's Comet in 1986, sending back images of the comet's nucleus and providing a wealth of new information on these visitors from the outer Solar System.

HUMANS IN SPACE

The first man into space, Colonel Yuri Gagarin of the former Soviet Union, orbitted the Earth in 1961. Since then numerous trips have been made into Earth orbit as well as nine flights to the Moon, six of which resulted in successful lunar landings.

Astronauts today have much more spacious craft to move about in and can spend much of their time in orbit in casual clothes, unlike the early astronauts who had to wear their bulky spacesuits throughout their missions.

It is now over 20 years since the last Moon mission and all manned flights have been restricted to Earth orbit. However, some of these flights can last for considerable lengths of time. Russian cosmonauts have spent almost a year in orbit in their space station, Mir. These long trips provide essential information on the long-term effects of weightlessness on humans. We will need this information if crews are to be sent on the long voyage to land on Mars.

The rocket-powered Manned Manouevering Unit, first tried out in 1984, gives astronauts the freedom to move around in space outside the space shuttle. The first astronaut to use one flew 100 metres (330 feet) out from the shuttle. Previously, astronauts were tethered to their spacecraft when they took walks in space.

Ancient astronomers believed that the stars were fixed to the inside of a sphere that circled the Earth and this idea of a celestial sphere is still used in mapping the sky today.

Opposite are some of the constellations that can be seen in the sky above the Earth's Northern Hemisphere. These are the constellations closest to Polaris, the Pole Star, which can be found in the sky near the celestial north pole, directly above Earth's North Pole. The constellations appear to turn about the Pole Star as the Earth rotates.

Among the interesting things to be seen in this part of the sky is the double star sytem of Alcor and Mizar in the constellation of Ursa Major, the Great Bear. Two of the stars in Ursa Major, sometimes called the Pointers, can be used to help you find Polaris. Also visible are Capella and Arcturus, two of the brightest stars in the sky.

On a clear night, where there isn't any artificial light to interfere with the view, the Milky Way can be seen running across the sky through the constellations of Cygnus, Cassiopeia and Perseus.

The Andromeda Galaxy, also visible under good conditions, can be found in the constellation Andromeda. At 2 million light-years, it is possibly the most distant naked eye object.

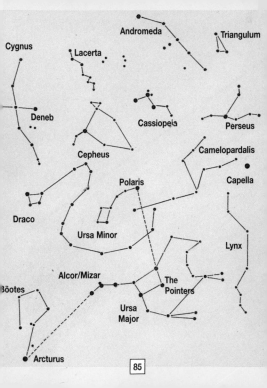

The constellations of the southern skies revolve around the south celestial pole just as the northern constellations turn about the north celestial pole, although there is no star like Polaris located at the turning point.

Many of these constellations were named by seventeenth- and eighteenth-century astronomers, which explains why some have the names of scientific instruments, such as Telescopium, the telescope, and Microscopium, the microscope, rather than being named after mythical heroes like the northern constellations.

Among the most interesting sights in the southern sky are the Large and Small Magellanic Clouds. These are in fact small galaxies, satellites of our own Milky Way Galaxy. The Large Cloud is about 160,000 light years away and the Small Cloud about 210,000 light years distant. A few years ago one of the brightest supernovae to appear in the last 400 years flared up in the Large Magellanic Cloud.

Also visible is Alpha Centauri, one of the brightest stars in the sky, and one of the closest to Earth.

In the southern sky the Milky Way can be seen passing through the contallations of Carina, Vela, Crux, Circinus, Triangulum Australis, Norma and Ara.

SOLAR SYSTEM FACTS

The Sun
Age: 4.5 billion years
Diameter: 1,392,000 km (865,000 miles)

Mercury
Distance from Sun: 57.9 million km (36 million miles)
Diameter: 4878 km (3031 miles)
Orbital period: 88 days

Venus
Distance from Sun: 108.2 million km (67.2 million miles)
Diameter: 12,103 km (7520 miles)
Orbital period: 225 days

Earth
Distance from Sun: 149.6 million km (93 million miles)

Diameter: 12,756 km (7926 miles)
Orbital period: 365.26 days

Mars
Distance from Sun: 227.9 million km
(141.6 million miles)
Diameter: 6726 km (4180 miles)
Orbital period: 687 days

Jupiter
Distance from Sun: 778 million km
(483.6 million miles)
Diameter: 142,984 km (88,784 miles)
Orbital period: 11.86 years

Saturn
Distance from Sun: 1427 million km
(887 million miles)
Diameter: 120,536 km (74,898 miles)
Orbital period: 29.46 years

Uranus
Distance from Sun: 2871 million km
(1783 million miles)
Diameter: 51,118 km (31,763 miles)
Orbital period: 84 years

Neptune
Distance from Sun: 4497 million km
(2794 million miles)
Diameter: 49,528 km (30,775 miles)
Orbital period: 164.79 years

Pluto
Distance from Sun: 5913 million km
(3666 million miles)
Diameter: 2284 km (1419 miles)
Orbital period: 248.54 years

LIGHT-YEARS AND MAGNITUDE

Astronomers use the light-year, the distance that a ray of light, travelling at 300,000 km/s (186,000 mph), covers in one year to measure the distances between stars. It is roughly equal to 9.5 million million km (6 million million miles). By this reckoning Proxima Centauri, the nearest star, is just over four light-years distant.

Astronomers call the brightness of a star or any other object in space its magnitude. The larger an object's magnitude the fainter it is. A magnitude 1 star is 2.512 times brighter than a magnitude 2 star and 100 times brighter than magnitude 6. A reasonable pair of binoculars will show stars as faint as magnitude 9.

THE TEN NEAREST STARS

Proxima Centauri: 4.3 light-years

Alpha 1 Centauri: 4.3 light-years

Alpha 2 Centauri: 4.3 light-years

Barnard's Star: 5.8 light-years

Wolf 359: 7.5 light-years

Lalande 21185: 8.2 light-years

UV Ceti A: 8.4 light-years

UV Ceti B: 8.4 light-years

Sirius A: 8.8 light-years

Sirius B: 8.8 light-years

THE TEN BRIGHTEST STARS

Sirius
Magnitude: - 1.46
Distance from the Sun: 8.65 light-years

Canopus
Magnitude: - 0.73
Distance from the Sun: 1200 light-years

Alpha Centauri
Magnitude: - 0.1
Distance from the Sun: 4.38 light-years

Arcturus
Magnitude: - 0.06
Distance from the Sun: 36 light-years

Vega
Magnitude: + 0.04
Distance from the Sun: 26 light-years

Capella
Magnitude: + 0.08
Distance from the Sun: 42 light-years

Rigel
Magnitude: + 0.1
Distance from the Sun: 900 light-years

Procyon
Magnitude: + 0.35
Distance from the Sun: 11.4 light-years

Betelgeuse
Magnitude: + 0.49
Distance from the Sun: 390 light-years

Achernar
Magnitude: + 0.51
Distance from the Sun: 117 light-years